A New Mind for a New millennium

Will Buttrose

GOKO
MANAGEMENT

GOKO Management
ACN 002 530 298

Level 8, 182-186 Blues Point Road
McMahons Point NSW 2060

Phone: (02) 9922 5334
Facsimile: (02) 9922 5343

ISBN 0 646326 65 1

Cover Design by Donna McClelland

Printed by Griffin Press

I dedicate this book to my father Charles Buttrose who in June 1997 turned 88 years of age. My father, due to family reasons, left school at the age of 14 but educated himself by reading widely — history, politics, music and autobiographies, authors such as Hemingway, Dickens and Shakespeare. From cleaning printing presses on a newspaper's production line he rose to become one of Australia's leading journalists and author of several books. My father has been an inspiration to me and helped me from an early age to develop my writing skills. My sister Ita and my brothers Charles and Julian hope our Dad is around with us for many more years.

Contents

Introduction

*Every dynamic organisation knows that change is the engine of growth. The change lies not in embracing this business tenet, but in anticipating, adapting to and generating fresh ideas that exploit change. (*The Trend Letter *Washington, U.S.A.)*

In 1995, I sat down and wrote a book which I hoped would assist people in achieving their dreams and their goals and objectives, for themselves and their families. Little did I know the success that book — *Economic Sunshine for the Rest of Your Life* — would have.

I have received hundreds of calls and letters from people asking me for more information on the subjects covered in the book. This was in addition to the many 'thank yous' from people, saying that they were so glad to finally have found someone expressing in print not only what they had felt, but who had clearly spelt out the foundations on which they had built their own success.

My first book discussed topics such as:

- Personal success
- The economy and how to understand it
- The massive changes confronting the world as we moved through the 1990s to the year 2000 — the beginning of the third millennium
- The downturn in traditional employment prospects
- The technology revolution and its impact upon our business practices and home-lives
- The future of financial security inherent within the growth of home-based business
- Goal setting and time management

The reaction to my first book clearly showed many people awoke to the realities of the harder business and working environment into which we have entered. The book set people talking and thinking about their current and future prospects. This reaction gave me a renewed impetus to widen my examination and interpretation of some of the key issues I originally discussed.

Especially important to me, indeed as a fundamental platform to my whole philosophy of life, is the need for people to take control of their own financial future; to set goals and objectives; to achieve such ambitions through hard work and forethought; and to be prepared to grasp opportunities when they present themselves.

I am hopeful that my books will not only be of benefit to you but also be of interest and assistance to your children. I am soon to celebrate my thirtieth wedding anniversary. With three children in their twenties I am very much aware of the enormous problems confronting our children, as they pursue their own careers and strive to achieve their personal goals and objectives.

As a 'baby boomer', I am aware of how lucky I was to commence my business career at age 17 back in the 'easy days' of the early 1960s.

These days there is virtually nothing easy for our children in the demanding and, at times, harsh work place in which we all find ourselves.

You and I must not forget the challenges facing our children. Their understanding of the topics raised in my books should help them prepare for the challenges that lie ahead.

One of the shortcomings of my first book was that, due to the desired size and format of the book, I was not able to include, in any meaningful way, the volumes of data collected and analysed which assisted me in its writing. A number of the issues were dealt with in an anecdotal way, but many of my readers expressed a desire to know more, to get into the research itself. Hence, in this new book, I have included numerous quotes and references which highlight the background to many of the key issues that I covered and the subsequent conclusions that I reached in *Economic Sunshine for the Rest of Your Life*.

New Opportunities

In the rapidly changing world in which we live, there are wonderful opportunities opening up to people which will assist them to convert their lifestyle and financial dreams into reality.

In this book, I will again emphasise the need for people to rethink their job prospects, and indeed their whole relationship with the traditional employment market. There is little doubt that nine-to-five jobs will continue past the year 2000 (not as many as there are today but nonetheless such jobs will exist) but by no means is any of us guaranteed to have such a job!

Let's have a brief look at what we will discuss in the chapters ahead.

Chapter one: I will explore the job prospects of the traditional nine-to-five company employee and analyse what the future holds. Change is going on all around us. It is inevitable it will affect each of us.

Chapter two: I will reassess the options open to the traditional nine-to-fiver and whether he or she wants to seize control of their own future and avoid becoming another unhappy statistic in the unfortunate ranks of the unemployed and unemployable! I will again stress that setting up one's own business is becoming an extremely viable alternative in the face of massive change and job losses.

Chapter three: I will examine more closely the idea of developing leveraged income, that is an income earning operation which, once successfully established, requires less and less of an individual's time but which, over time, offers either a fixed or increasing income stream. My previous book talked of my father and the ongoing royalty income he developed through writing a successful book. The income stream flowed for many years even though his work effort ended when he wrote the final chapter of the book. I'm glad to say that the option of developing ongoing, leveraged income is still open to each of us, and being able to write bestselling books is not a prerequisite!

Chapter four: I will whet your appetite for what might be, by relaying true life, success stories of people who have generated significant monthly incomes through their own home-based businesses. Indeed, all around us there are many success stories, people who have backed their own judgement, started their own businesses, proved the 'negative and never take an opportunity' type people wrong, and through their individual efforts moved forward to success. Indeed, I will document a major new trend, white collar professionals turning to entrepreneurial opportunities so as to secure their future. No more boring meetings, traffic snarls, rude bosses, complaining clients, impossible deadlines or golden handshakes for them. Maybe such a new direction and lifestyle would be welcomed by you!

Chapter five: I will ask you to dream, to sit down, think about your life and decide what really could be (indeed what should be) the future direction of your life. But of course, here your fears, and quite natural fears, will emerge. Am I good enough? Intelligent enough? Talented enough? I will spell out for you that there are some golden opportunities to make a leveraged income by just being you, but by being all you can be!

Chapter six: In moving towards my conclusion, I will focus on image. Image is an important theme in the 1990s and it will become more so in the new millennium. People will want to deal with successful people — with people they feel confident and happy to deal with and who present themselves as professionals. In a media driven society, everything about you and your business must be governed by the words image and success.

Bill Clinton was not elected again so much for his honesty or his stability as a married man; he won the image race! I will offer some practical advice on how you can both present yourself with a positive image and manage a home-based business — with equal aplomb!

I trust that this book is a 'new mind for a new millennium' and will be received by you with the same enthusiasm as my previous book. I hope that it will provide the impetus for you to critically examine your future income and employment prospects under your current job and then, in turn, begin the process of developing your own guaranteed income for the future through a part-time or full-time home-based business.

To those of you who are on this path already, I commend you, and trust you will find here some words of encouragement for the wise choice made for yourself and your family, and that you will share your success story with others.

A New Millennium

A new millennium is quickly approaching. Some people will succeed and thrive in it. Some people, by not understanding and facing the challenges, will be thrown on hard times. Some people will fail despite their best efforts. Where will you be? Read on and discover what many people recognise as the recipe for success in the new millennium — discovering and developing a new mind!

Chapter One

Jobs — Here Today, Gone Tomorrow

There is a crisis coming. The crisis is that of global unemployment or under-employment of some 800 million people. And that figure is likely to rise sharply between now and the turn of the century as millions of new entrants into the workforce find themselves without jobs — many victims of a technology revolution that is fast replacing human beings with machines in virtually every sector and industry of the global economy ... Redefining opportunities; and responsibilities for millions of people in a society absent of mass employment is likely to be the single most pressing social issue of the coming century. (The End of Work *Jeremy Rifkin)*

A cultural change is currently sweeping the world and such change will gather momentum as we move into the year 2000 — into the new millennium.

The world has changed over a series of major economic stages spread over 2000 years. We began with hunting and gathering, became agrarian, have been in the industrial age over the past 200 years and in the last two decades have entered the information age.

The world has entered a new age. The information and technology revolution is impacting on every industry and, in turn, every employment sector. Human beings are being replaced by computers and machines, as companies strive to be competitive and profitable.

"On the eve of the third millennium, civilisation finds itself precariously straddling two very difficult worlds, one utopian and full of promise [for the employed], the other dystopian [imperfect social system] and rife with peril. At issue is the very concept of work itself. How does humanity begin to prepare for a future in which most formal work will have passed from one human being to machines?" (*The End of Work* Jeremy Rifkin)

There are hundreds of examples of the mounting pressures faced by the corporate sector which, if it is to survive, must embrace new technology to the detriment of jobs.

"When JMR Design started trading less than three years ago ... [the] company found they could streamline their business to a staff of three by using state of the art technology. A decade ago, they would have needed ten people to do the same work ... Ten years ago, it would not have been possible to operate a business with a structure as lean as ours. In JMR's case, technology has replaced staff, allowing us to do more work with less human resources'." ("Digital Staff Cuts Costs" *Dynamic Small Business Magazine* June / July, 1996)

Ongoing technological change will continue to transform the traditional office and the traditional job. Consider the following statements by a small business owner.

"Technology is very important for a small business like mine ... The company is able to do so much more work with the tools we have. We wouldn't be able to survive without it ... Time savings and increased efficiency are the sorts of ways that technology has become increasingly important for my business ... Machines are becoming faster, smarter and a lot smaller. This impacts on the amount of space you require. Business is going to be completely portable. The work environment of the future will virtually be in your briefcase." ("The 21st Century Office" *Small Business Magazine* June / July, 1996)

The hard facts are that life is changing at an unparalleled rate. You and your children must be alerted to these facts because the information age is going to affect each and every one of us. Traditional jobs, traditional ways of handling our finance and traditional ways of life are changing. The old ways will never return.

Changes in the Finance Markets

When our parents bought houses, the banks were the only providers of mortgage finance — the traditional lenders. But by the late 1990s, a dramatic change had swept the market.

According to an earlier report by the Sydney based and highly respected financial institution, Bain Securities (now incorporated within Deutsche Morgan Grenfell Securities), "More than 60% of all mortgages in the United States originate outside the traditional banking system." In Australia, Bain predicted non-bank mortgage origination could reach 50% of new business by 2000. ("Counting on Financial Advice" *My Business Magazine* February, 1996)

In fact, with the explosion of Aussie Home Loans (which by mid-1997 had provided $5 billion in home loans), with life insurance companies now active in the mortgage market and with the rapid growth generally of the secondary mortgage market, the banks' share of the mortgage market is likely to be even lower than Bain suggested.

Lifestyle Change — Cafes

In my early years, a cafe was a place where you ordered a cup of coffee and read the sports columns of the morning newspaper.

Today: "Cybercafes are popping up all over the place, where patrons can pay a flat hourly fee to surf the net from the comfort of their chair. One of Sydney's newest cybercafes, *Well Connected* in Glebe, offers customers one of its 14 multimedia work stations for $12 an hour." ("Would You Like 8mb of Fries With Your Burger, Sir?" *My Business* February, 1996)

Job Security

"Downsizing. Rationalisation. Optimisation. Call it what you like, but thousands of employees are being offered a variation on the golden handshake in the form of voluntary redundancy packages." ("A Fortune Down The Hall" *Personal Investment* December, 1996)

"The death of the global labour force is being internalised by millions of workers who experience their own individual deaths, daily, at the hands of profit-driven employers and uninterested governments. They are the ones who are waiting for pink slips, being forced to work part-time at reduced pay, or being pushed onto welfare." (*The End Of Work* Jeremy Rifkin).

The Business Sector

Frank Hiob, a management expert, who has advised American presidents and consulted to some of the largest corporations in the world commented: "Three years ago I saw change as incremental; now I see it as accelerating ...We live in an age of paradigm shifts, and they're happening all round us all the time. It's led by technology. The power of the micro-chip is doubling every 18 months, with a corresponding reduction in price. This has changed the way we do business." ("The Shock Of The New" *Home Office & Business* Vol. 2, No. 1).

"Such is the way of the future: big companies will be asset-rich, but with small workforces. Most of the brainpower will be accessed by 'outsourcing'. Business will become more entrepreneurial — it will be easier to innovate than to compete. Traditional professions will be increasingly challenged by innovations and there will be a plethora of new jobs which would have been unthinkable a generation ago." ("The Shock Of The New" *Home Office & Business* Vol. 2, No. 1).

But where will we find these jobs? Let there be no doubt — there is a future for people faced with the prospect of losing their current job in the years ahead. We shall explore these prospects in the next chapter.

There is now virtually only one certainty that you and I can predict. It is the certainty of change. "Twenty years ago, an American author, Alvin Toffler, wrote *Future Shock* — a promise (and warning) that the pace of social change would accelerate, and that the only certainty was change. At every tier of human existence, we would face increasing disorientation. The challenge was to manage change." ("The Shock Of The New" *Home Office & Business* Vol. 2, No. 1)

"In an era where jobs are about as scarce as successful government policies, small business is increasingly donning the super-hero cape to rescue young and old ... who have done time on the dole queue." ("A Neis Alternative" *Home Office & Business* Vol. 2, No. 1)

Indeed, what we are seeing in Australia, the U.S. and elsewhere around the world, is that small businesses in these challenging times are thriving while big business continues to retrench and struggles to achieve satisfactory profits.

Become an Entrepreneur

In the U.S., the youth of America have risen to the challenge and have actively set out to start their own businesses. "Today's young Americans have earned the dubious achievement of being perhaps the first generation to experience a lower standard of living than their parents. Not content to live down to those expectations, 69% of high school students say they want to start their own businesses, according to a national Gallup organisation survey on entrepreneurship. 'It's a total change in attitude,' says Marilyn Kourilsky, vice president of the Centre for Entrepreneurial Leadership Inc. in Kansas City, Missouri, which sponsored the study. 'High school students see all these layoffs and just don't believe that the government or the corporate world is going to take care of them ... [Kourilsky believes] generation X is going to be the entrepreneurial generation. These kids are very hopeful'." ("Great X-expectations" *Entrepreneur* February, 1995)

The message is clear. Starting your own small business may provide the successful strategy for your future.

Chapter Two

Income in the New Millennium

> *On 1 January 1996 the first of Australia's 5 million baby boomers turned 50. They are turning 50 at the rate of 700 a day ... With retirement staring them in the face and only 12% saving for that goal, few of the 'first wave' boomers have any hope of reaching the estimated $1 million each household will need to retire comfortably.* (Sydney Morning Herald *30 November, 1996).*

There is no such thing as job security. In the old days a person could spend their entire working life with just one, or perhaps two, employers.

Be aware of the potential insecurity of working nine-to-five for someone else. This feeling of job insecurity was a contributing factor to low levels of consumer spending in Australia in the mid to late 1990s. People refused to spend because they were not confident of their long term employment prospects.

No business, no matter how relevant it is, or how well established it appears to be, is immune from the pressures of international and domestic competition. Nor are they immune from the pace of ongoing technological change. No employer, no matter how well intentioned or humanitarian, can avoid the business necessity to keep costs to a minimum, to remain competitive, and to review the profitability of each and every business operation within the corporation. Companies have to be profitable if they are to expand and move ahead in the competitive market place. The bottom line is that labour costs are one of the cost components, if not the major component, of all companies.

If profits are under pressure and if conditions demand action, then the inevitable action more likely than not sees people join the unemployment queue. It is a new millennium and the rules for the game have changed. Employer loyalty to their workers is almost a thing of the past.

Cost of Employees

Most of Australia's major publicly listed companies have been forced by economic conditions to continually review their operating costs and the products and services they manufacture or provide. They have to decide whether or not some product lines or services should be abandoned and with that decision jobs go.

Boards and management of companies do not enjoy the pressures placed on them by their banks and their shareholders. However, the facts of life are that in this world of dramatic change the above mentioned actions are symptomatic of the way things are in corporate life and will be in the new millennium.

The fact is that companies look at costs every day. Management must report to the board and explain why profits are not growing at their budget levels. The banks, which provide credit to the companies, question the profit and loss figures. If profits are too weak then banks may decide to cancel the current loan facilities and ask for immediate repayment. The shareholders, whose investments in the company are critical to its future capital raising programmes, expect to see adequate profit announcements and dividend payments. If not, shares are sold and the company's share price can collapse.

When profit figures are analysed, it is the human labour costs which often loom large as a problem area. From the sweeper on the factory floor to the production manager in the manufacturing plant, labour costs, including wages, overtime, superannuation, worker's compensation, holiday leave loading, sick leave, and so on, are enormous. When the decision is made to cut costs then employees from all parts of the corporation, from cleaning staff to management, find their job is on the line. As staff are retrenched, or accept voluntary redundancy, extra work load is often placed squarely upon the shoulders of those who remain. People are expected to work harder and, for those remaining in employment, this is often an unwelcome consequence of the above decisions.

Let's not kid ourselves, work does not evaporate into thin air when employees disappear. Reality tells us that efficiency measures do not always equal one-for-one job losses, and those who remain employed end up carrying the slack. People find themselves working harder and for longer hours with no increase in their pay packet. Many people have decided to seek a better alternative.

The Human Toll

Some people might suggest the above is an exaggeration. For those who are sceptical and who work for a large company, I suggest a simple test: examine your company's occupational health assessment report for the past ten years. Almost without exception, companies are experiencing disastrous results in stress-related absenteeism and work related insurance claims. Insurance companies are writing reports every month on the ever-increasing claim figures related to stress.

Also, it is no accident that the so-called 'yuppie flu', which leaves young people in the Australian and international corporate work place lethargic and without energy, has coincided with one of the most stressful periods of job market upheaval in corporate history. Let's be realistic, job pressures are not going to ease in the years ahead.

Conditions in the corporate world are difficult and will remain so. People are recognising these facts and are looking for new options. They are saying, why wait to be retrenched or suffer stress and other physical problems working longer and longer hours, when new opportunities are available. Opportunities that could enable you to take control of your own future and to create your own job in the new millennium.

Four Basic Options

If you are a person who has decided to take control of your future, then you have the following four basic options on how you can better secure your job and income earning capabilities:

1. Find a new job protected from the ravages of corporate downsizing and industrial change.

2. Become a consultant to your existing employer.

3. Buy into an existing business which can guarantee you an income into the future.

4. Create a new mind for a new millennium and start a low-cost, low-risk home-based business, which will provide leveraged income for the years ahead.

Let's take the opportunity to explore these options a little further.

1. Find a new job

Finding a new job these days can be exciting and challenging, but it is certainly not as easy as it used to be. I remember when I left school at the age of 17 and went looking for a job in the accounting area. I wrote to five of the jobs advertised, was granted three interviews, was offered two jobs — and then chose the one I wanted. This is certainly not the case for today's school leavers.

Indeed, many highly employable and previously successful people are finding that the job market is extremely tight. There are people today who, having earned in excess of $100,000 in the late 1980s, are being rejected from the same type of job which is today paying $60,000 a year.

However, suppose you find a new job and it appears to provide good prospects for the future. The problem remains that no matter how rosy it all looks now, change is the one thing you can count on in the new millennium. Businesses with markets and customers today are finding, in an increasingly globally competitive economy, that their markets are disappearing quicker than cobras in a mongoose farm. Working for others will remain fraught with danger, because fundamentally you are at the mercy of someone else. You are not in control of the situation.

2. Consultancy

The second option for the person seeking to take control of their own destiny is to set up a home-based operation, consulting to your current / previous employer. This is known as outsourcing and is becoming increasingly popular with employers as a way of farming out work to an external workforce. Typical outsourced work includes accounting, book keeping, debtor control, computer work. For this option, it's always best to let your boss initiate such a move!

This is not to be confused with working for an employer from home. Some companies have the facility of offering employees the chance to work from home, which is sometimes referred to as 'teleworking'. This is a trend already evident in the U.S. and one which will gather momentum in Australia. In this technological and computer driven world, working from home is very practical and obviously very cost effective for the corporate employer. There is no need for your own office, no need for support staff and indeed, as the trend develops, no need for corporations to have a big expensive office building in the city. However, the person working from home is still a company employee and is subject to the labour market whims described earlier.

These observations are supported by independent commentary. "During the next century, as work becomes more portable and self-contained, the need for a traditional office space is likely to decline for many businesses. It's a trend that has already emerged. Last year an estimated 7.6 million American workers, 5% of the total U.S. Workforce, were 'telecommuting' — using fibre optic cable and modems to minimise actual travel to and from a central office. More and more people are working from home, exchanging a concrete road for the information superhighway. Why? Because telecommuting is said to be easier, more productive, gentler on the environment and allows the worker more lifestyle choices. As many as 33 million Americans and two million Australians could be telecommuting by the year 2010." ("The 21st Century Office" *Dynamic Small Business* June / July, 1996)

I read an article recently which illustrates this trend in future employment. "If [the manager] wants to get in touch with any of [her] 200 staff ... She has to reach for the phone or the keyboard ... Interest in telecommuting (working at home and keeping in touch by phone, fax, modem, voicemail or the internet) is certainly on the rise." ("Why working from home makes long-term sense" *Business Review Weekly* 18 September, 1995)

There are many good reasons for this, one of the most obvious being, "Work is not what it was ... An office does not have to be designed as a factory, and the cost of all that space is not worth the convenience of seeing and shouting (at someone). Focused intelligence, the ability to acquire and apply knowledge and know-how, is the new source of wealth ... Most other people who work in their own space in an office eventually will work from home ... The main advantages to telecommuting are obvious: flexible working hours to allow family obligations to be met and less time spent commuting." ("Why working from home makes long-term sense" *Business Review Weekly* 18 September, 1995)

Outsourcing is also a popular alternative to employers, because it means they can wash their hands of what is known as salary plus, plus, plus. This means that you currently cost your employer more than just the $50,000 a year you are paid. The fact is that showing up at the office every day, you are expensive to run.

"The tendency of big business to cut back on staff in the recession gave rise to all kinds of home-base consultants who are still in demand." ("Why working from home makes long-term sense" *Business Review Weekly* 18 September, 1995)

"Downsizing and outsourcing by big business are helping create a growing army of small business consultants ... The major outplacement and career management firms have found that 20% of their displaced clients are opting for self-employment and that outsourcing of some services by 35% of major Australian companies is creating a healthy demand for consultants." ("Turning the Sack into a New Job" *Sydney Morning Herald* 10 September, 1996)

"Outsourcing is a trend that should increasingly benefit cost-effective and innovative small businesses. Large and small businesses alike are under constant pressure to reduce and / or contain costs, and will contract out increasing parts of their work. As a result, low overhead operations will become increasingly competitive." ("The 21st Century Office" *Dynamic Small Business* June / July, 1996)

Therefore, outsourcing offers an attractive alternative, because now the employer pays you — the consultant — only an hourly rate, no doubt higher than previously, but nowhere near the level of what it cost to have you as an employee, that is, wages plus workers compensation, superannuation, sick leave, holiday leave loading and so on. However, when work is slow, you can find yourself with nothing to do and no pay either. Therefore, think twice about this as a real alternative. I have known many people who made great money for a year or two 'consulting' to their previous employer, but eventually the work dried up, or, more likely, someone leaner and hungrier offered the same consultancy services at half the price.

On balance, options 1 and 2 are not real solutions. But what about option 3, buying into an existing business?

3. Buy into an existing business

Despite one's best intentions, buying into an existing business can be both difficult and time consuming. For one thing it is possible to buy into a business which appears to be running well and profitably only to find when the owner leaves, the business collapses.

If you are thinking of going into business, then stay ahead of the information game, and get your facts straight. " ... The lesson for those of us who are either in or planning to go into business is that there is a pool of important information we must expose ourselves to in order to improve our small business pictures. The better our businesses are in terms of knowledge, the lower the small business failure rate will be." ("Chalking up experience" *Home, Office & Business* Vol. 2, No. 1)

Existing businesses require solid research. They can be good value, but you would have to be very careful. The highways and byways of the 1980s and 1990s are littered with the tragic stories of many well intentioned, ambitious people who bought an existing business and lost their entire life savings, including their house.

In addition, existing businesses are not immune from the vagaries of the economic cycle or the global economy. Just recently, near where I live, supermarkets have been granted permission to open, up to 24 hours a day. This is not a revelation in some parts of the world, but it is to many local corner shopkeepers who are now realising what this will probably mean to their trade, their livelihood and their families. Many people, having bought such businesses in good faith, could find their life savings ravaged and their future shattered.

What about franchises? After all, we are told constantly that this is a wonderfully safe option for starting your own business and securing your own financial future. Let's consider franchises for a moment.

An article appeared in the February 1996 edition of *My Business* magazine, entitled "Where does '90s opportunity knock?" It outlined some of the key prospect areas for aspiring entrepreneurs in the new millennium. Of interest to you and I are the comments on franchises.

Director of Ernst & Young Entrepreneurial Services in Melbourne, Don Brumley, believes franchising is 'the key ongoing trend' which offers opportunities for those looking to run a business. "Many people who take early retirement, for example, are leaving with an amount of money which is appropriate for entry into a franchise ... Franchising also appeals to those younger workers who may find themselves retrenched and don't have the specific business skills necessary to venture out on their own ... For someone younger who is retrenched ... they need a [business] idea where risk levels are minimised if they don't have the business expertise ... [Franchising is] the area with the lowest risk and is the most affordable for these people when they're looking to start up a business. We see it as an area which should grow quite strongly. Increasing at an annual rate of 17%, the franchise industry is expected to continue growing at this pace, providing business opportunities as a consequence." (*My Business*, February 1996)

This is a pretty positive assessment of franchising, and indeed there are many wonderful opportunities which require very little training. Many franchises are also inexpensive, though the cost is never negligible, and in that sense they are still a risk. One of the keys to the above quote is that it is honest about the financial requirements for setting up a franchise. They do require an element of capital outlay. What do you do if you don't have such capital? Are all the doors closed to you?

The Realities of Franchising

In the U.S. people attempting to purchase franchises are finding that: "Financing a franchise involves weaving through a maze of options. Many franchises rely on old standbys — friends, family, and home equity loans. They often sink every last cent into their businesses and pledge their personal assets to the hilt." ("The Road To Wealth" *Success* December, 1995)

It is interesting to note also that Don Brumley of Ernst & Young indicated that franchising is 'low-risk' not no-risk. I was intrigued recently to read that McDonald's franchise owners in Australia have been threatening action against the U.S. parent company for failing to look after franchises. It seems that McDonald's franchises are being set up at such a rate that they are killing each other off, being located too closely together for the size of the market. This should register another warning about franchises.

Franchise Fatigue

These days it seems it is more attractive to develop a business of your own than franchise it. Many clever people have realised the possibility of earning their own leveraged income by 'selling' franchises, and this in itself should issue another warning.

Consider, as an example, the owners of a successful, self-created business in Queensland. The male found himself unemployed with a $7,000 redundancy. He hit upon the idea of washing 'wheelie bins' and made a success of it door-to-door. Now they are franchising his concept.

"Realising they had a hit on their hands, [they] decided that the best way to expand was by offering franchises.

Placing small adverts in newspapers and business magazines, [the business] has quickly spread throughout Queensland. And now the couple is starting to market Australia-wide ... Overseas expansion is now on the cards with offers to take the concept to the U.S." ("Bin busters" *My Business* February, 1996)

Clearly the owners have moved a long way from washing garbage bins, and who can blame them? Having adopted a new mind, they have realised the secret of leveraged income and will leave the 'wheelie bin' washing to others. We shall have reason to return to this theme later.

"In spite of the dangers of buying a franchise and the high level of costs involved, the industry is growing at an amazing rate and will continue to do so. It is estimated that ... the franchising industry in Australia generates $43 billion in annual sales turnover, employs 280,000 people and continues to grow at a rate of 14% as businesses and households outsource more activities and services." ("Queensland: Perfect for Small Business" *My Business* February, 1996)

This phenomena is true of the whole world as people become more and more perturbed with traditional employment and look for new ways to create their own future. "All indicators suggest that franchising is on the upturn, both in Australia and internationally. Worldwide franchising sales per country averages $18.3 billion ... A country like Japan has a turnover figure of $86 billion" ("Franchising Now" *Dynamic Small Business* June / July, 1996)

Here are the comments of a franchise consultant. "As a franchise consultant who has been observing and participating in the development of franchising for 20 years, I have seen a lot of new franchisees trumpeting their virtues only to disappear in subsequent years, whether quietly or not so quietly ... [of 260 franchisees identified in 1984] ... Only 51 franchisees, or 20% of the originals listed, are still operating." ("Taking the mystery out of franchising" *Sydney Morning Herald* 4 June, 1996)

There are many well intentioned people losing money in the franchising game. I cite as an example the following case. "Carpet steam cleaning is one of those businesses that has attracted people who have taken packages from secure jobs. Newspaper advertisements, under the business opportunity section promise an income of $1,000 a week for an outlay as small as $10,000 and virtually no training. So 'Bill Brown' hands over his money, gets a steam cleaning machine and perhaps a cheap van and waits for the phone to ring. It may ring for the first few weeks, but then it stays quiet and he is left with no income and his savings gone. Disillusioned, he tries to sell his machine and faces up to one of life's hard lessons: he's been ripped off." ("Steam Cleaning Can Burn Fingers" *Personal Investment* December, 1996)

So, be warned — while franchising remains an option for many, it is not necessarily the most attractive option for taking control of your own financial future. The facts speak for themselves, as 20% or more of all franchises worldwide fail. (Figures from "Franchising Now" *Dynamic Small Business* June / July, 1996)

4. Create your own home-based business

If franchising is not necessarily the most attractive option, then a fourth option is the creation of your own home-based business — an option which has worked for hundreds of thousands of people around the world.

Some interesting facts

Consider the following facts about the 100 fastest growing businesses in Australia in 1996.

"One-third of these businesses were started from home ... You do not need much to start a fast-growing business. The vast majority had between $5,000 and $20,000 and a fifth had less than $5,000." ("100 Fastest Growing Companies" *Business Review Weekly* March, 1996)

"[In Australia] by the year 2000 as many as 12% of Australian homes could house a business according to some estimates." ("Tax Office Eyes Home Business" *Dynamic Small Business* June / July, 1996)

"By the year 2000 some 49% of Americans will be working from home." ("No Place Like Home" *Home Office & Business* Vol. 1, No. 1, 1995)

In home-based businesses "People are doing everything and anything: home arts and crafts, service industries and professional businesses ... Working from home is a wave sweeping the world and brings the possibility for more of us to take personal responsibility for ourselves and our income and allow us to combine work and family as never before." ("No Place Like Home" *Home Office & Business* Vol. 1, No. 1, 1995)

"Studies overseas show that people who work from home are up to 80% less stressed than colleagues in an office. This leads to increased productivity (instances between 20% and 100% have been reported) and quality (up to 10%)." ("Why Working from Home Makes Long-term Sense" *Business Review Weekly* 18 September, 1995)

An advertisement appeared recently for a book on home-based business. Here is what it said. "In the United States, one in three members of the total workforce work at home either full or part-time. More than 40% of workers are self-employed and work part-time and around 20% work at home for others as 'telecommuters'." ("The Home Business Bible" *Home Office & Business* Vol. 1, No. 1)

There can be no argument. The development of home-based businesses will be a growth industry in the new millennium.

More Facts & Figures

The statistics on home-based businesses are astounding: "It appears, according to figures produced by the Australian Bureau of Statistics, that more and more people are working from home. In 1993 it was estimated that some two million Australians were fortunate to work from home in some capacity. These people included an increasing number of people who were self-employed or partners and employees of small companies." ("Laying the Foundations" *Home Office & Business* Vol. 1, No. 1)

These figures are backed up by the findings of the *Personal Investment* magazine. "The total number of Australians doing at least some work from home has increased over the last few years — the percentage of the work force in this category has risen from 23% in 1989 to 26% in 1995." ("Welcome to the Work-wide Web" *Personal Investment* December, 1996)

Benefits

And just consider some of the benefits of a home-based business for a moment. "It's cheaper to work from home and allows many entrepreneurs both old and young to try out their ideas without the high risk factor. Above all, it is often the flexibility that appeals as the seven day week can be utilised fully to provide work time, family time and leisure at the choice of the worker and not dictated by the Monday to Friday, nine-to-five ethic of the 'boss'."

"Working from home is a wave sweeping the world and brings the possibility for more of us to take personal responsibility for ourselves and our income and allow us to combine work and family as never before. The challenges are enormous but the resulting feelings of personal satisfaction and the possibility of improved family relationships and cementing our local communities make it an exciting and viable option in today's world." ("No Place Like Home" *Home Office & Business* Vol. 1, No. 1)

A new life at home

The impact upon our home lives cannot be underestimated. My three children are now grown up and in the work force, but many parents today would love the opportunity to bond more closely with their children by working from home.

Consider the following example. "She was 'happily retrenched' from [her company] ... And when that happened her first question was, 'What am I going to do now?' ... She set up shop for herself ... [She] explains that operating her own business has given her the opportunity to be at home with her son and yet keep her business life going — the best of two worlds."

("Business Booming Baby Blooming" *Home Office & Business* Vol. 1, No. 1)

The editor of a popular business magazine wrote recently that new businesses are being started by "Mothers who want flexible hour arrangements to accommodate responsibilities to children. This has swelled the numbers in home-based business ranks. Adding to this group are those women who feel that lack of promotion in the corporate world has made it a sensible strategy to create their own business. Capable men are also inspired by these reasons. Since the recession the number of white collar workers who have taken restructuring packages to open up a business has been enormous ... Now, more than ever before, individuals are selling their services as a business instead of as an employee." ("From the Editor's Desk" *Starting Your Own Business* 1995)

Another article said, "One of the main reasons the business is more cost-effective than many of its competitors is that its overheads are low. 'Our office is well equipped, has good kitchen facilities and doubles as our home as well ... One of the major benefits is that we don't have to travel anywhere. It gives you more time — time for work and for leisure'." ("Designing a Lifestyle" *Australian Small Business & Portfolio* March, 1996)

Of course, you don't have to start your own business to get these benefits. As I said earlier, tele-commuting to your job also allows the same flexibility. People spend, "Less time commuting to and from the office and [spend] more time with [their] children ... [telecommuting offers] ... Advantages for women, who have been largely unable to combine the demands of work and family since the demise of the cottage industry in the mid-1850s." ("Why Working from Home Makes Long-term Sense" *Business Review Weekly* 18 September, 1995)

Why a Home-Based Business?

Let's have a look at some of the many benefits that are associated with a home-based business.

People cite many reasons in wanting to create their own home-based business. A poll in *Home Office Computing* revealed the following reasons people gave for working at home.

1. I wanted to be my own boss (72%).

2. I wanted less routine in my life (56%).

3. I wanted to change my life (43%).

4. I wanted to do more interesting work (41%).

5. I disliked the corporate world (35%).

6. I wanted to spend more time with my family (33%).

It is very easy these days to do business in the world from the comforts of your own home. "With the technological revolution — especially in telecommunications and on-line technology — there is a whole range of business functions which can be performed without having to find business premises outside of the home. Home-based businesses now range from traditional 'cottage industries' to professional service providers offering great flexibility, balance and lifestyle opportunities." ("Queensland: Perfect for Small Business" *My Business* February, 1996)

All of this demonstrates that if you decide to set up a home-based business that you must not be out of step, estranged or disoriented. Indeed you would be joining a U.S. led world trend. The establishment of a home-based business alongside your traditional job is a terrific way of securing your financial future, while generating that much-needed extra monthly income.

What Type of Home-Based Business?

I would suggest that you look for a business which fits with the changing circumstances of the new millennium. For example, "For years, food manufacturers and retailers have recognised that a growing number of consumers are not prepared to slave in the kitchen preparing meals.

Convenience was one of the biggest trends in the food industry during the 1970s and 1980s, as manufacturers rolled out a parade of increasingly convenient products. Convenience remains an important trend in the 1990s." ("Coming to Grips with the New Consumers" *Business Review Weekly* 17 July, 1995)

In the new millennium, therefore, one of the keys to success will be getting in on a business which will make purchasing consumables more convenient for people. "The growth in sales of ready-to-go food is being driven by time pressures, laziness, a shift away from the kitchen as the heart of the home, and the realisation that do-it-for-me food can cost the same as meals prepared at home ... Paid work will account for less of people's time; because of the increase in leisure time, greater value will be placed on leisure activities. People will outsource repetitive and boring chores, including cooking." ("Coming to Grips with the New Consumers" *Business Review Weekly* 17 July, 1995)

Life will change in the new millennium. The key is to get on the right side of that change.

I leave you with some good advice, from a successful home-based entrepreneur, on what to do if you agree that a home-based business, developing your own income flow, is a good idea. "If there is a singular suggestion I could make to someone who is thinking about a home-based business, it is to speak to someone in the same situation." ("Beyond the Comfort Zone" *Home Office & Business* Vol. 2, No. 1)

May I suggest you seek out someone you know who has developed a successful home-based business and speak to him or her about your income earning capabilities. You have nothing to lose but you may discover an opportunity that suits your ambitions.

Chapter Three

Leverage in the New Millennium

The types of enterprises that are creating the new jobs ... As in the other nations that have entered the infotronics age [i.e. the information age], fewer new jobs are to be found in the industrial age corporations [i.e.. the large Australian companies].

The growth employers are to be found in the medium and small (new entrepreneurial) firms, more and more of whom are franchising or networking for economy of scale purposes ... Opportunities are to be found in different occupations, industries, locations and types of enterprises ... It's where you look that counts ... Why not start your own business as many of our forebears did? (Phil Ruthven, Chairman IBIS Business Information Pty Ltd)

We have talked at length about four basic options open to you for securing your financial future in the new millennium. The title of this book should give you the clue as to how I see the future unfolding for the success-minded in the new millennium. Your success will depend upon your ability to adapt a new mind set, to open your mind to see new opportunities and then to grasp such opportunities when they present themselves.

It is possible, isn't it, to see things but not really see them? It's just like looking into one of those three dimensional illustrations and seeing only a blur of dots and not the image behind. That is very much like success in the new millennium.

There are some incredibly simple opportunities available for people who are willing to have a go at them. Some of these opportunities have been around for years, but perhaps were not fully understood by all. But in the new millennium, many clever people will cash in on home-based businesses which produce leveraged income in simple ways.

One of these home-based businesses is called direct selling or direct marketing. It is this business which provides cheaper products to the consumer by selling products direct from the manufacturer to the consumer without the involvement of the middle man, that is, the retail store, the corner store, or the supermarkets. You think it's not going on?

Consider the following. "Home-shopping through the internet or television will grow incrementally." ("The 21st Century Office" *Dynamic Small Business* June / July, 1996)

"Of the *Fortune* 500 companies in the U.S., 70% [have] web sites." ("Softly-softly Treading into Cyberspace" *Dynamic Small Business* June / July, 1996)

The fact that major U.S. companies included in *Fortune* magazine's 500 top companies have identified the world-wide web as a place to set up shop should tip off the astute entrepreneur as to where the future of shopping and distribution lies in the new millennium.

"Retailers had one of their worst Christmas sales in 1996. The retail industry faces a big challenge — a consumer revolution lead by smart shoppers who want more from their dollar ... Today's customer will shop around to find the best deal ... in the background, too, is the threat from new sources such as direct mail and on-line shopping via the internet and pay TV." (*Sydney Morning Herald*, 11 January, 1997)

"The aims of most companies now on the internet are to expand their marketing potential and incorporate their profile ... Those who have already established a presence on the internet ... have assumed an attitude that necessitates adaptation to change." ("The potential of the internet" *Management* June, 1996)

How Are They Doing It?

"Internet marketers are ... Securing an audience for their marketing and sales messages. By offering information or entertainment-based value, many internet marketers are drawing huge audiences to their sites." ("What the Internet Means for Marketers" *Database Marketing* No. 14: August, 1995)

Is It Really Happening?

Let me quote to you from the *Business Review Weekly* magazine of 11 September 1995. "Significant will be the marketing of a whole range of services that will be carried over interactive cable networks, including banking, shopping, education, investment, gambling, travel and software. If you are in any of these businesses, you need to develop a strategy to cope with the boost [of] the number of [people] connected to an electronic network and able to participate in the wider range of services".

"The other day the proprietor of an Australian liquor shop was stunned to get an order for Australian wines from an American via the internet. As more of our businesses link to local cable networks, they will discover the wider world and will begin to reap the advantage of being world pioneers in interactive cable. So our companies will be able to export their products and services to customers around the world, using new marketing methods." ("First Glimpses of the New Era" *Business Review Weekly* 11 September, 1995)

In 1995, the *Database Marketing* magazine commented that "today over 40 million people in over 120 countries are connected to the internet and other on-line services."

This represented phenomenal growth. However, these figures are already outdated with the release of figures in early 1997 showing that in the U.S. alone, 50 million Americans are now on the internet. The message should be clear to everyone.

Forward thinking Australian companies have moved with the times. As early as September 1995, the *Internet Australasia* magazine wrote that the car manufacturer Toyota is 'on-line'.

Car manufacturer Toyota is even 'on-line' in the new millennium. "Toyota is the first vehicle manufacturing company in Australia to make use of net technology with its home page ... As well as providing an information service to Toyota owners, the Toyota on-line site is an interactive brochure of Toyota products including latest vehicle models and accessories ... When the Toyota home page was launched in late June this year, net users were able to view the latest sporty Rav4 which itself was released only a few days earlier. Toyota on-line acts as both an advertising and customer service site and will soon allow customers to arrange test drives of new vehicles and make service appointments on the net." ("Toyota On-line" *Internet Australasia* September, 1995)

Even the banks are getting onto the home-shopping internet phenomena. "71% of small business owners have a computer. While 91% of this group have heard of the internet ... Within a decade, or maybe even sooner, you and your bank manager should be catching communication waves together on the internet. Through the 'net', banks will be able to connect with their customers. They will be able to advertise products and services. You will be able to complete transactions, go over documents, update records and even interface with your banking officer ... Basically we are waiting for the world to feel at home with the internet so that the full potential of this 'virtual' market place can be realised. When that happens we will be better buyers of banking products. This will save time and, better still, money." ("Banking on the Internet" *Home Office & Business* Vol. 1, No. 1)

Businesses and people that succeed in the new millennium will be those on the cutting edge of the new technologies and new opportunities for the distribution of products. "Commentators ranging from Peter Drucker to IBIS Business Information's Phil Ruthven emphasise the emergence of the information age, in the wake of the industrial age. The growth industries will be those at the forefront of the changes taking place in society, whether it is telecommunications or personal services." ("Editor's note" *Business Review Weekly* 18 September, 1995)

The following article on Mr. Barry Diller, a man who took home-shopping onto the worldwide computer-net, appeared in the *Sydney Morning Herald*, but derives ultimately from the *New York Times*. It said that he intended to transform the profitable "Business of home shopping by sending it into cyberspace ... by combining the direct-marketing muscle of home shopping network ('HSN') with the instant access of the internet, Mr. Diller said, his company would soon be able to reach the affluent, professional consumers who long eschewed TV-based electronic retailing ... The internet could expand HSN's business from thousands of transactions a day to millions. HSN ... is now ploughing $U.S. 10 million ... into a redesign of its web site that will enable the service to take orders and deliver products around the clock ... Commerce has already established a foothold on the internet, with retailers selling $U.S. 254 million worth of goods and services on-line last year."

"America On-line, CompuServe, MCI Communications and the Microsoft network have all started centralised shopping areas, intended to look like electronic shopping malls with shopfronts, for the various merchants offering their wares." ("TV Shopping Chief Heading into Cyberspace" *Sydney Morning Herald* 21 May, 1996)

"The laying down of nationwide information super highways, and the opening up of hundreds of new cable channels with interactive capabilities, promises a flood of home-shopping services. Companies are investing huge sums of money in the new home-shopping television networks, convinced that shopping without a store is likely to be the next growth market in retail sales." (*The End of Work* Jeremy Rifkin).

You and I know that most business trends commence in the U.S., or some other major industrialised power, and then some years later enter Australia. The rapid growth of computer technology including the internet will soon explode into Australia. Businesses and people who accept this inevitable development and the changes it will bring to the buying and selling of goods will position themselves for success in the new millennium.

The internet will give competitive businesses the chance to market globally and, as this happens, consumers will benefit from competition and direct selling. I noted with interest the following recent comment from an influential magazine.

"If your business isn't on the web yet, it should be ... This fastest growing section of the global computer network represents perhaps the most cost-effective way businesses can advertise their products or services. Once a company has set up a 'web site' presence for a modest outlay, the site can be maintained at a minimal cost while the company goes about getting its message out."

Remember that by early 1997 there were 50 million Americans on the internet. However, while the growth of internet users has surpassed everyone's predictions, the conclusions reached by the *Business Opportunities* magazine in 1995 are still valued.

Business Opportunities in 1995 noted that understanding "the strategic implications of the internet has become a hot item on boardroom agendas ... With an estimated 30 million current internet users, and predictions of up to 100 million users by the end of the decade, now is the time for business professionals to learn about the value of the internet as a strategic business tool."

Some of the above quotes obviously refer to retailers, nevertheless the benefit to the consumer will be the same in the long run as the high costs of the middle man, the retail store with its costs of land, building, staff and stock levels, are replaced by the electronic shopping mall.

This desire of producers to bring products direct to consumers is called direct marketing. And it is direct marketing opportunities via the internet which are being grasped by the business sector.

"There will be in the 1995 / 96 financial year about 23,500 small business internet customers, about 90,400 home customers and 42,000 big business customers." ("Net News" *Australian PC Review* October, 1995) This trend has only just commenced.

Now, where is this discussion leading us? Does one have to advertise on the internet to do direct selling? Not at all. This chapter is about leveraged income, and one of the easiest ways to develop leveraged income in the new millennium is through becoming involved in the direct distribution of products.

Direct distribution may sound strange and out of the ordinary now, but it may not be in the new millennium. I was not surprised to read recently that Heinz Australia, the mega baby-food distributor, is now selling its products direct to the public, cutting out the middle man.

You probably recall the hoo-ha caused by Heinz Australia's announcement that it was going into direct marketing in a big way. "Direct marketing is simply the smartest, most cost-effective means of reaching this particular target market." ("Behind Heinz's $3.5 million move into direct marketing" *Database Marketing Magazine* No. 14, August, 1995)

With severe competition, profits under continual pressure and sales growth difficult to achieve, manufacturers and wholesalers will, in the new millennium, go direct to consumers by any reasonable means they can find. This keeps costs down and allows businesses to be competitive. This will be achieved by direct marketing or direct distribution

A concept that has existed for 30 years or more in direct marketing is that of network or multi-level marketing, or interactive distribution. This process allows people to commence a home-based business involved in the direct distribution of products to consumers. The beauty of this system is that, done correctly, it will permit a person to develop an on-going, leveraged income for the rest of their lives.

Leveraged Income

What is leveraged income? Leveraged income is income which falls virtually into what we might call royalty income.

As mentioned earlier, my father wrote several books which were quite successful. One of these books was turned into a movie. From this 'home-based' venture, which was a non-risk, no-cost venture, my father received regular royalty income which was ongoing for years and years after he completed the writing of the book.

Consider the power of this type of income. You write a book once; it may take months or even a year or two but afterwards, all you have to do is whatever is necessary to continue ongoing sales. This may include promotional appearances, book signings or whatever, but the workload is now very light in relation to the ongoing income. Some months you do nothing, but income is still accumulating on your behalf.

Can this be done in direct-marketing? It certainly can. The development of a professional business network, of people just like you, who long to develop an ongoing, leveraged income for the rest of their lives, is one of the simplest means by which to develop a successful home-based business in the new millennium.

Will direct marketing work? In the context of a move by increasing members of people to home shopping, consider the following. "Many business people don't want to do their own shopping, and there is an increasing demand for home shopping, home delivered food and meals and personal products. People pay for these products to be brought to their door or sent through the mail ... There are many directly sold cleaning products, appliances [and] car products ... Home-order shopping here is a recent trend. Americans have been doing it for years and we're only just discovering it."

"How does it work? The distributor sends the customer a catalogue of all the ... products available from the supermarket and the customer ticks the products and the quantity they want. They can either phone, fax or mail the order through to the distributor. The order is delivered two or three days later ... Sign up recruits and receive a percentage of their sales. Multi-level ... marketing has many benefits for the avid salesperson." ("Direct Marketing and Selling" *Home Office & Business* Vol. 2, No. 1)

This move to home-based shopping was highlighted in my previous book. What is being described above is the development of a powerful network of like-minded people, all desiring success, all pulling toward the same goal. It is something you can do from home, while keeping your nine-to-five job, but the income will help protect you should you fall victim to the changing job market in the new millennium.

Women Move into Home-Based Business

A home-based, direct selling business operation, is something a husband and wife can successfully establish and which can also involve the children. Most interesting, as far as home-based businesses go, are the astounding statistics for successful businesses developed by women. In my opinion, women of all ages, including mothers taking care of children at home, are a vastly undertapped resource in our society.

Personal Investment, in a study on home-based business owners, discovered that "Most are female. They number more than double male home workers. Females employed at home account for 6.4% of all employed females.' ("Welcome to the Work-wide Web" *Personal Investment* December, 1996)

My Business magazine found that "Women own about a third of the estimated 757,000 small businesses in Australia. They also start new businesses at twice to three times the rate of men ... Forecasts ... [are] that women will own 50% of small businesses by the late '90s." ("Taking Care of Business" *My Business* March, 1995)

These figures were supported by *Business Opportunities '95,* "According to the Employment and Skills Formation Council (1994), women are establishing small businesses — especially in the area of self- and home-employment — as much as three to four times faster than men." ("Women are Dominating Small Business" *Business Opportunities '95* September, 1995)

However, women striving to achieve success in their own small business operation often are confronted by important family problems. An article on Australia's top 50 women in business, found that, "According to the Victoria University Study, the majority (62.7%) of women entrepreneurs were either married or in a ... [long-term] relationship. Of those, 43% cited lack of time for family and / or relaxation as their greatest conflict. The next highest category was difficulties with child care at 12.3%. A number of women (7.4%) said they felt guilty when devoting time to their business at the expense of their family." ("Australia's Top 50 Women in Business" *My Business* March, 1995)

These results would no doubt be the same in the U.S. and around the world. Typical small business ventures often bring such problems. However, a home-based business overcomes these difficulties and allows time to meet the conflicting schedules of work and family.

"Running a business from home enables women to take control of their professional careers while providing flexibility to work around family commitments such as looking after children." ("Smooth Operator" *Home Office & Business* Vol. 2, No. 1)

Women who happily went out to work in the 1970s and 1980s are now returning to work from home. Many of these women will find what they are looking for in a home-based business. One of the great opportunities lies in direct marketing.

"Women are now returning to work from home in their thousands. Twice the proportion of women to men who run small business operate from home. It's not surprising that one of the reasons women find the home office so attractive is the improved quality of life. A 1994 study by the Australian Bureau of Statistics showed that an increasing number of families are attempting to combine work and child caring responsibilities by converting part of their home into an office." ("Smooth Operator" *Home Office & Business* Vol. 2, No. 1)

"Women need more money for retirement than men because they live longer ... Once upon a time letting your husband handle the finances was as normal as a hat and white cotton gloves — 80% of married women will spend a decade on their own ... Young women are starting to take a more active role in organising their own finances — buying their own homes and putting money aside for retirement." (*Sydney Morning Herald*, March 1997)

Why Should You Pursue a Home-Based Business?

Is it all worth it? Should you pursue a home-based business with a leveraged income? Is direct marketing a growth industry? What have you got to lose? Nothing! But you have a lot to gain.

As far as direct marketing is concerned, a report released in May 1997 by the Commercial Economic Advisory Service of Australia estimated that direct marketing advertising grew by almost 15% to $6.3 billion in 1996 — it is indeed a respectable and growth industry.

"It would be with great reluctance and an impossibly outrageous salary that I would ever consider working again for someone else. A home business equals an absence of office politics, and being answerable only to yourself. I am responsible for my own workload and my own success." ("Beyond The Comfort Zone" *Home Office & Business* Vol. 2, No. 1)

It would be a dream come true, wouldn't it!

So in the new millennium, working from home could be a great alternative for men or women individually or a husband and wife working together. The reality is, as I will illustrate in the next chapter, that many people are successfully working from home.

Chapter Four

Leaders of the New Millennium

Direct marketing takes many forms — among them direct mail, telemarketing, infomercials, home shopping, TV channels and internet promotions. All of these direct marketing formats are exploding in growth around the world ... The five most profitable non-U.S. markets today are Canada, the United Kingdom, Australia / New Zealand, Japan and Germany.

Already firmly established in the U.S., home shopping is exploding around the world. Home shopping channels are very popular in Japan where about 70% of Japan's 125 million people have made a catalogue purchase. Home Order Television, *Germany's first home shopping channel, already reaches 7.6 million homes in Germany and Austria. Home shopping channels are already established in the Czech republic, Poland, Hungary, Latin America and is expected in Russia in 1998. (*The Trend Letter *March 1987)*

Much of what I write about in this chapter may be revolutionary to you. Some of it you may not believe. But I assure you it is true. As we approach the new millennium, there are already many people earning substantial amounts of money, sometimes in addition to a well paid full-time professional job, through truly leveraged income.

These people have worked hard, put in the hours and worked through the challenges of commencing a new business. They have made the decision that they would not be overcome by the massive changes sweeping the world. They were determined not to become hit and run victims as the information super-highway passed through their offices and through their homes. These people took a gamble, threw themselves into direct selling and ... well, read on and see what happened.

"South Carolina state senator Mike Rose graduated from Harvard business school and New York University law school and has taught entrepreneurship at the state college in Charleston. After losing money during seven years in politics, he became a [direct marketing] distributor ... Now Mike Rose has a reported personal income of more than $10,000 per month." ("The New Elite" *Success* December, 1995)

Welcome to the new millennium, where people from all walks of life, from a diverse range of backgrounds including wealthy, educated professionals, have decided to stake their claim for leveraged income and a more certain future.

"Anne T. Coughlan, associate professor of marketing at Northwestern University's Kellogg Graduate School of Management in Evanston, Ill., confirms there is a new elite in network marketing. 'A lot of people are being right sized out of their jobs,' she says. 'They don't have the guarantee of employment their parents had and these well-educated people want to be in control of their destiny. They would like to be entrepreneurial'."

" 'These companies (network marketing companies) harness, at the individual level, people's eagerness to work to benefit themselves,' says senator Mike Rose. 'You're able to be your own boss and have more opportunity than you could possibly utilise efficiently and do good for people in the process'." ("The New Elite" *Success* December, 1995)

What About Network Marketing?

"There is a new class of entrepreneur breaking into what used to be considered a working class industry. White collar pioneers are bringing established professional and social networks, new technologies, and new credibility to network marketing. These are people who already have career options and adequate incomes. The attraction here is the promise of becoming both financially independent and achieving control of their own lives." ("The New Elite" *Success* December, 1995)

There are so many examples we might draw on of entrepreneurial type people who have made a success of what is called 'direct / network marketing' or 'interactive distribution'. Here are a few more:

"Lloyd and Peggy Morris of Austin, Texas had spent ten years building ... their real estate business ... They decided to make a change in 1989, when Peggy saw real estate mogul Donald Trump on television's *The Tonight Show*. 'He was asked what he would do different if he had it to do over again,' she recalls 'and he said he'd get into network marketing'." ("The New Elite" *Success* December, 1995)

This is an interesting observation from a man who has ridden the roller coaster ride of property investment but has made hundreds of millions of dollars in real estate. But Trump had obviously thought through the simple issues involved in direct selling / network marketing.

"Network marketing — also called multi-level marketing, or MLM — is simply a distribution system for goods and services. The most venerable and well known network marketing companies include[s] $6.3 billion-a-year Amway Corp. ... Some would say MLM is creating a whole new marketplace 'outside the box' of TV advertising, store fronts, inventory, and middle men and has the power to render the conventional retail world obsolete." ("The New Elite" *Success* December, 1995)

One thing is certain, the lifestyles of these leaders of the new millennium are second to none. Consider the following comments on Lloyd and Peggy Morris from *Success* magazine.

" 'We have more free time than we've ever had,' says Lloyd. When the Morrises recruit other professionals, they talk about the control over time. 'Often when we're talking to a corporate executive, he'll say, Do I have to go to meetings? When we tell him no, there's a sigh of relief at the other end of the line.' After a distributor reaches a certain level of sales, he can retire from selling and still collect commissions on sales from his organisation [true leveraged income]. 'Lloyd and I could retire right now,' says Peggy, 'and our income would increase anyway, because our organisation will probably still be growing'." ("The New Elite" *Success* December, 1995)

How does that sound to you? The leaders of the new millennium are clever people. They have developed a new mind to deal with life's changing circumstances and they have decided to find new ways to get what they want from life.

"Because multi-level marketing or MLM builds fortunes by accumulating residual commission income [read leveraged income] from large downlines, it is set apart from most professional work. Doctors are a classic example of non-leveraged people — highly paid hourly workers ... They're paid only when they work ... When I started talking about network marketing, some of the doctors were surprised and a few of them laughed. When I explained the economics, though, none of them laughed." ("The New Elite" *Success* December, 1995)

The leaders of the new millennium are not dummies. They know the value of a dollar and how to get one. They also know how to take control of the number of hours they wish to work to ensure their financial security for the future.

Another leader of the new millennium noted that, "[There are] six criteria to define the perfect opportunity: no retail, no store front, no collections, no receivables, no inventory, and plenty of residual [i.e. leveraged income.]" ("The New Elite" *Success* December, 1995)

Let us consider the ramifications of this for a moment. When we talk about multi-level marketing, we are talking about a business opportunity that:

- Requires a small initial outlay of funds of a few hundred dollars. Therefore, if for whatever reason the business is not a success or you decide not to continue with it, you have not had to outlay any significant amount of money to get the business up and running

- Does not require leased space for a shop or office
- Does not involve carrying stock
- Still affords one a leveraged income for life

It sounds too easy; surely there is a downside?

"In the past, multi-level marketing or MLM was not a big draw for professionals because [of its] reputation. In 1993, Kellogg marketing professor Anne Coughlan set out to discover how MLM really works. She surveyed 150 companies to measure distributor's productivity and how they are paid. She found real opportunities for individuals in MLM because network marketing rewards performance so directly." ("The New Elite" *Success* December, 1995)

It would appear there is no downside. Let me quote you a tongue-in-cheek description of this opportunity which I read recently. "A stranger walked into the employment office of a large company and announced to the manager 'I've decided to work for you.' The manager's head snapped up from his work. The unexpected visitor continued without waiting for a response. 'But there are a few things you need to be aware of before I start.' The stranger began slowly to explain, 'First, I will be setting my own hours, I won't be working every day of course, and when I do decide to work it will only be for a few hours at a time'."

"The manager was in stunned silence. While his jaw hung open the visitor politely added the requirements. 'As a representative of this company, I assume you will provide excellent products at below competitive prices. In addition, you must offer incentives to my contacts that will make it very (and he stressed very) worth their while to consider your products. When asked, I'll take time to explain the details, but beyond that the company must do the balance of the work. The company must provide facilities and staff to look after inventory, order processing, money collection, taxes and product delivery. And even though I won't risk any of my money, I still require substantial compensation for a job well done'."

"The manager's face regained a little of its colour now, suspecting that this most unusual visitor was probably sent by some practical joker in the company, he half raised his hand to ask a question but the visitor didn't notice and carried on. 'In three or four years I may decide to retire. However, if the company continues to do business with my past contacts, I will expect my income to also continue. One last point ... I have a few friends who may be looking for similar positions and you must accept anyone I refer to you.' The visitor took a deep breath, smiled and finished with, 'If you have no problems with my requirements, I'd like to complete the paperwork now'."

"By now the manager was enjoying the joke. 'I don't know what planet you're from but I've never heard of a position that good,' he roared. Then leaning forward, he sarcastically added, 'If you know where to get that kind of position, you can count me in and probably half the staff here too!' The stranger leaned forward and, eye-to-eye with the manager, very quietly said, 'As a matter of fact I do. Let me introduce you to someone I know who has this unique opportunity.' And the manager stopped laughing. 'This position does exist. Would you like to learn more about it?' " ("The Manager Stopped Laughing" *Australian Business & Money Making Opportunities:* Nov. / Jan., Vol. 6, No. 4)

The stranger was describing direct marketing.

It's no laughing matter really. Some people will survive in the new millennium, indeed thrive, because they have chosen to create their own leveraged income.

"I believe this is the finest financial opportunity you will ever have in your lifetime. If you do this, you will never have to do another job in your whole life." ("The New Elite" *Success* December, 1995)

Why does direct selling / multi-level marketing / network marketing / interactive distribution work so well?

"In MLM ... You invest time rather than capital. The more time you invest, the more return you get for each increment of time." ("The New Elite" *Success* December, 1995)

Now, is direct selling the only way to operate in the new millennium? By no means. "It started just over a year ago. I was a night cleaner working rotten hours and not at all happy with what I was doing. My wife ... and I decided that the only way we were going to get ahead was to start taking control over our own future and with three children we wanted to be able to give them the best start in life we could. We came to the conclusion that owning and operating a small business would at least give us a light at the end of the tunnel, something we can work towards. This business had everything we hoped for. We decided to run it part-time from our garage. It was unreasonable to expect a new venture to support us straight away, so I still worked nights. Trading started in January 1995 and our business took off like a storm." ("The Right Choice" *Australian Small Business & Portfolio* March, 1996)

The above is yet another example of two leaders of the new millennium — a husband and wife team successfully launching a new business. Having a new mind, they attacked their problems aggressively and created their own future in a home-based service business.

Many people question whether direct selling is reputable. Consider the following statistics covering direct selling distributors and the annual sales being achieved.

"Worldwide direct retail sales are estimated at $U.S.68 billion, and there are more than 17 million distributors. The U.S. alone has 6.3 million distributors (up from 5.7 million one year ago), who accounted for $U.S.16 billion in sales last year (up from $U.S.15 billion). Countries where direct selling is strongest include Japan ($U.S.30.3 billion), Taiwan ($U.S.1.7 billion), and Korea ($U.S.1.3 billion). Malaysia and mainland China are coming on fast ... Household names such as Bausch & Lomb, Coca-Cola ... GE, IBM, ... Sharp, ... AT & T, MCI, Sprint, and Xerox have products or services distributed in part through direct selling." ("The New Elite" *Success* December, 1995)

And note the above are 1994 / 95 figures and growth in direct selling has accelerated since then.

The Australian Experience

According to the Direct Selling Association, direct sales turnover in Australia in 1995 / 96 climbed to $1.6 billion compared to just $150 million in 1975 / 76.

Direct selling organisations in Australia now number 38 and the number of distributors has climbed to 600,000.

The figures from the U.S., Japan, Asia and Australia confirm that direct selling, or multi-level marketing in its many forms, is a secure, reliable business. After all, it brings together the two major trends which will become increasingly evident in the new millennium. "Direct selling represents the confluence of two titanic trends. The first (trend) is what we might call the 'transaction cost revolution.' As technology reduces transaction costs, farming out functions to specialists becomes more and more efficient ... Network marketing companies farm out their sales, marketing, and management functions to thousands of independent contractors. 'The second trend is the home-office revolution: as computer and communications technology make it more practical to work from home, more people do so." ("The New Elite" *Success* December, 1995)

Another successful person in the new millennium put it this way: "I wanted something I could do on my own, where I could call the shots." ... He researched 500 companies in a variety of fields before deciding on network marketing. "It's never seemed like work to me. I could sit with my one-year-old in my lap, the TV on low, and talk on the phone. I was in heaven." ("The New Elite" *Success* December, 1995)

Let's summarise a few points here. Really, at the end of the day it does not matter what kind of leveraged income business you choose to pursue provided that:

- You know a few people in the same business who have made a success of it

- You know people in the same business who can help you develop yours

- Your choice of business has a low start up cost

- You are not involved in excessive risk

- Your present job is not threatened by your home-based business

- You wholeheartedly believe in what you are doing, you have the courage of your convictions and you are willing to work hard

You don't necessarily start out with the objective to replace your present job. Ideally, what you want to do is to secure a financial future where you will not need a job! What would you be doing if this was a reality for you? In the next chapter I will address that question, but let me add one final word.

I believe interactive distribution / network marketing / multi-level marketing presents an opportunity for you to create your own home-based business. It is not the only opportunity, nor is it necessarily the right one for you. But this book is about you creating a new mind set, being open to opportunities, and taking a real, honest look at such opportunities while acknowledging that dramatic change will accelerate in the new millennium.

You may not wish to start the type of business discussed in this chapter. That is, of course, your choice. However, in the new millennium, the key is to be open to every possibility; to have a look at things and see what will work for you. It is important that you be sufficiently motivated to change your own situation and circumstances, so that you take control of your future and ensure that you will not be a victim in the new millennium!

May I suggest, in conclusion, that if you know someone who has taken control of their own future, maybe even the person who gave you this book to read and who is developing a successful home-based business, that you talk to that person about your future income earning potential.

Chapter Five

Believe in Yourself

As your own boss you will also need the sense of self worth to assert your own boundaries, determination, motivation and persistence to go beyond self doubt, plus an understanding of how your mind really works. (Home Office and Business *Vol. 2, No. 1)*

What does success mean for you? What do you want to achieve for yourself and your family in terms of lifestyle? Are you close to achieving it? If not, why not? What is stopping you from getting there? What decisions have you not yet made to achieve your objectives?

The real key is to decide what you want. Then set yourself a plan to achieve these objectives. It is easy to become negative and to believe the doubters who say you cannot do it. But do you really want to be one of these people — a non-achiever?

People struggle with self doubt and a lack of self confidence. Many people lack motivation and ambition but not you.

There are at least seven key factors which deter people from starting a new business venture and these are:

- The risk factor
- The time factor
- Lack of knowledge
- Lack of confidence
- Fear of personal failure
- Working capital requirements
- Believing in the myth of job security

Let us examine each of these factors in a little more detail.

The Risk Factor

Many people lack the commitment to consider starting a new business because they are concerned that should the business not succeed they could lose a lot of money.

Each of us is very much aware of the business disaster stories that we have read in the newspapers, heard on the radio, watched on television or even seen in the lives of some of our friends.

Typically, these stories revolve around a person or, on many occasions, around a married couple who have outlaid a significant amount of money to start a new business, to open up a franchise or to become a partner with another person in an existing business.

People often consider new business ventures around the age of 40-45 and in many cases the start up capital to commence the business takes a large part of their savings. Once a new business is started and once the initial major capital outlay has been spent, there is the inevitable pressure to continue to pump more money into the venture even if the business is not making money. It is a hard decision to reach that the business is a failure and should be shut down. Within a year or two a person's entire savings can be lost.

Clearly there are major risks in becoming involved in a new business. I do not blame people for looking and understanding the risks involved and deciding not to proceed any further. The message is clear. The risk of losing all your life savings at a late stage in your working life is not a risk which should, generally, be taken.

The Time Factor

Many people when presented with new opportunities insist, "I don't have the time," and use this as an excuse to not consider any aspects of a new business proposition put to them.

I know that, in the competitive environment in which we all work, each of us is working longer and longer hours, taking work home at night and working on the weekends. The thought of taking on any further work responsibilities is quickly ruled out.

I fully appreciate these circumstances. In the new millennium stress and illness caused by long hours of work will become increasingly more common. However, I also believe that most of us can manage our time better and more successfully. It is a matter of prioritising one's working day and if this is done then it is not out of the question that some time can be allocated to a new business opportunity.

Lack of Knowledge

It is in most people's natures to feel intimidated by new opportunities which require them to go past their comfort zone. They have genuine concern about their lack of knowledge, skill and experience relating to the new business opportunity. I fully understand this reaction — the fear of the unknown.

However, it is always easy to say no. But most of us, I would suggest, have never really stretched our full capabilities. To simply reject a business opportunity on the basis of feeling that one does not know enough about the business and therefore cannot do it, is to assume that you can never grow, learn or adapt to change — which simply is not true.

Lack of Capital

As already discussed, many new business ventures require start up capital — an initial investment to get the business going, and often an amount that takes a large bite out of one's savings.

There are many people who in these difficult times live day by day with no savings accumulated at all. Each day is a struggle, to meet the mortgage repayment, the car repayment, the school fees, clothing for the children and so on.

Whether you have savings or not, the decision not to enter a business proposition because of a lack of capital is valid. What each of us must do is calculate what available financial resources we do have which in turn will enable us to decide on the business venture to which we are able to commit.

Lack of Confidence

Some people do not believe in their ability to achieve.

They look at others who have started a new business, and built up a successful and profitable operation, but then say to themselves I could never be like them. Others say that successful people have simply been lucky and add that they could never achieve similar success for themselves.

All of us, at some stage in our lives, have questioned our ability to meet a challenge or take on a new responsibility or promotion at work.

In my own business career, I have moved from accounting (my first job included winding up one of the partner's clocks and buying him his lunch every day) to corporate lending, to money markets, to corporate mergers and acquisitions, to economics and to funds management.

Each of these steps in my business career presented me with new challenges, new obstacles and new fields of endeavour. From the office clerk in the accounting firm to the general manager of a bank, I always believed I could succeed. I accepted the challenges and reached down inside to find the right levels of self confidence to successfully tackle each new career opportunity.

A lack of confidence can deter people from making career decisions. We should take the time to develop our self esteem and our confidence levels. You don't want to be one of those people who lets a good opportunity go by because you don't believe in yourself.

Fear of Personal Failure

Some people have the confidence to start a new business but decide not to do so because of the fear of failing. These people feel that failure is the end of the world. They go through life only attempting to do those things that carry no risk whatsoever and are guaranteed to be successful.

That would be ideal if one could operate in this manner. The fact is all real business decisions have an element of risk, an element of the unknown and the potential for failure.

Most wealthy, successful business people have in their lifetime entered some business which carried the real possibility of failure. There would be no entrepreneur alive today who has not accepted such risk. Indeed many of today's wealthy entrepreneurs have during their careers seen one of their business ventures fail, have learned from the experience and have moved on to bigger and brighter opportunities — failure can often be an excellent teacher.

No one wants to fail. Provided that the risk of failure cannot result in a major loss of one's savings and assets, then fear of failure is not a legitimate reason to ignore a business opportunity.

No Working Capital

When approached to enter a new business, many people would immediately say no because the very first thing that comes to mind is that they will be required to put up some initial working capital. As the majority of Australians have very little savings, the immediate answer to the business proposition is negative.

To be forced to raise borrowings from a bank to provide the required working capital, which in most cases requires mortgaging your house is, in most circumstances, an option I would not recommend.

If a business proposition requires a significant injection of start up capital, and if you do not have a pool of savings or investments, then lack of working capital is a valid reason not to proceed any further.

Myth of Job Security

Finally, many people reject a business proposition because they feel secure in their existing job environment and don't wish to take on any further responsibilities or challenges.

But how secure are they? When I left school in 1961, many of my friends joined a bank. A job with a bank was seen as a job for life. Not a very trendy job but a good, solid, safe career which would see one through to retirement.

How things have changed. Between 1992 and 1997, 32,000 people lost their jobs in the Australian banking sector — some security!

As I have commented before, in the new millennium there is no such thing as job security. To simply reject a new business opportunity on the grounds that one has a secure job is not practical and does not acknowledge the difficult times that most people will experience in the job market in the years ahead.

So what type of business opportunity is available and which of the seven key factors are realistic reasons to not proceed. A good business opportunity would have the following characteristics:

- Minimum start up capital requirement and no need for any further injection of money

- A business that permits you to determine how much time you commit to it

- A business in which you can be trained through a network of support and experienced people

- Through the above support, a business in which you can build up your self confidence

- A business which has limited down side and therefore limited risk of failure
- A business which can operate in addition to your existing full-time job

As we discussed in chapter 4, there are such businesses. Each of us has the responsibility to stay alert to such new business opportunities which if successfully pursued can contribute to securing our future.

Chapter Six

Deal Yourself a Winning Hand

*To sell well, he [Zig Zigler] maintains, you have to do three things. Firstly, have an intimate knowledge of your product or service. Secondly, have an absolute conviction about the quality of what you're selling. Thirdly, back it all up with persistent hard work. He says the 3 P's should not be forgotten. Do what you do professionally, politely and pleasantly. (*Australian Small Business and Portfolio *March, 1996)*

It may be that by now you have made the decision to develop a home-based business. In most cases and in its initial growth phase, this will be an addition to your existing full-time job. However, the foundations for the success of any business, whether it be part-time or full-time, is to be professional in all of the aspects relating to the business operation. Let us briefly run through the essential steps which need to be taken to successfully set up and run a small business operation.

The Business

Obviously, you must firstly decide on what type of business you are going to establish. What products or services are you going to sell or provide. You must be confident that the business can be successful and will provide a service or product which is in demand now and will continue to be in demand in the new millennium.

Knowledge of Product

Having decided what type of business you will operate, you must then become fully knowledgeable about the product or services you are selling or providing. This gives you the essential confidence to go out and promote your business.

Target Market

The next key is to draw up a list of individual names or companies to which you will sell your products and services. This is your target market.

Having identified your target market you need to commit yourself to making a fixed number of contacts or marketing calls each month. Depending on your time availability, I would suggest at least around 20 new contacts per month. Remember, success is not often easy to come by in the early stages of a new business. Do not lose confidence in yourself. Persistence and a belief in yourself is what is required.

Finally, know your prospective customer. If you understand the person's occupation, background and family circumstances you can work out what key personal factors you can build into your selling approach. In other words, every potential customer needs to be treated as an individual and your selling approach will not be a totally standard one but will vary from person to person.

The Initial Contact

First impressions are critical to success in selling. The telephone is likely to be the first point of contact. From this first contact, people will form impressions of you, your professionalism and the potential success of your business.

Whether it be a telephone call or a face-to-face meeting, it is essential that you rehearse what you are going to say. I have given speeches to major corporations and professional groups in Australia, the United States and Europe. No matter how confident I am in what I am going to say, I rehearse each speech at least two if not three times before the day of the presentation. I practice out aloud, make amendments to the text and make sure I am comfortable with the flow of my speech. Rehearsal is one of the keys to successful presentations.

Referring back to telephone contact, often you will want your prospective customer to ring you. It is not very professional to take business calls in your kitchen with the children running around in the background. Preferably, you should install a dedicated business line into your house and if possible into a room that is away from the living area. Professionalism is the key here.

The First Meeting

Having successfully arranged an appointment from your telephone call, the next essential step is to arrive punctually for this all important first meeting. To set a meeting at 8:00 p.m. and then arrive at 8:10 p.m. blaming the traffic or the children is simply not good enough.

Depending on the type of business, my rough rule of thumb would be that a business presentation should entail 20 to 25 minutes to explain the business and another 10 to 15 minutes for questions and answers. Anything longer than this and you can lose the interest of your prospective customer.

You should know from your notes, the background of the people you are calling. The first few minutes of the meeting should be to encourage some personal conversation about them and yourself. This is so important in establishing some relationship. If they have children and you also have children, some comments on school or whatever can establish this personal link.

If your home-based business is a part-time one, then look for the opportunity to talk about your full-time job and its responsibilities. This can often add credibility to yourself and to your presentation.

Then commence to explain clearly and in a professional manner your business proposition. Be professional but avoid being either too serious or too familiar. Ask if there are any questions and be clear, accurate and precise with all of your answers.

Remember, people are successful in selling because they can strike a common chord with a potential client and leave that person with the feeling, " I would like to do business with that person."

Follow Up

Ideally, you will have a business card to leave with a potential client. Your last words, at your initial meeting, should encourage the potential client to ring you, or let them know that you will get in touch with them during the next week.

Office

If you are running a home-based business, then you need to set up an office at home in a room where you can carry on your business in a professional manner.

As the *My Business* magazine said in its March 1995 edition, "When working solo in a home office, one of the great challenges is presenting a professional image and being contactable. For the home business, telecommunications is the key".

Therefore, to meet these standards you will require some of the following:

- A dedicated telephone line
- A mobile telephone with message taking / paging service facilities
- A facsimile machine
- A personal computer and printer
- A photocopier

Existing Clients

Having successfully developed a target list, you must dedicate real time to ensure that your existing clients are happy. It is no good spending all your time marketing or prospecting for new clients only to find existing clients become dissatisfied or disillusioned and sever the relationship. Long term existing client relationships is one of the keys to long term business success.

Administration

Finally, you must ensure that all proper accounting records are kept, details of income earned and receipts for payments are filed, and all tax deductible expenses can be verified to the satisfaction of the Commissioner of Taxation.

Many a small business has failed due to poor book keeping or when it is suddenly issued with an amended taxation bill from the Commissioner. In addition, if you are not keeping accurate figures, how will you know how your business is performing?

The Successful Business

If you address all of the above matters, then you will set the foundations for establishing and running a successful small business operation. You will have dealt yourself a winning hand by combining a new business strategy with a disciplined set of standards. You will have created for yourself a new mind for the new millennium.

Postscript

The world is changing at a faster rate than any one of us can predict or comprehend. It is imperative that each of us explores the opportunities available to us in the new millennium.

Each of us is given chances in life to set our direction, achieve our dreams and ensure our longer term financial security. I have given you the information you need to comprehend the changes occurring and to set a new course for yourself and your family.

Look at the opportunities around you, including those discussed in this book. Start your own business in whatever area of endeavour best suits you. Commit yourself to being successful, and be professional and honest at all times.

It is now more true than ever before. Do not put off to tomorrow what you can, indeed must, do today.

The time is now. The future has arrived. The new millennium is upon us.

I sincerely extend my best wishes to you and your family for the future, and to your success in creating your new mind for the new millennium.

Will Buttrose

Will Buttrose

Will Buttrose's career in financial markets and banking spans over 30 years and has included postings to London, the United States, South Africa and Hong Kong. His working experience has been quite diversified, having included senior management positions in banking and finance covering corporate lending, money markets and foreign exchange, economics and funds management.

Will has been acknowledged as one of the best known and most highly respected business and financial counsellors in Australia, with an exceptional talent for communicating his views in an interesting and informative manner. Whether addressing the boards of large corporations or speaking with mass audiences on radio or telelvision, Will is able to interpret financial matters in a language understood by all.

Will has addressed business conferences in the U.S., Switzerland and England and has written monthly econmomic/money market newsletters for two of his banking employers which were voted the best newsletters of this type in the Australian financial sector.

Will's depth of business experience and his involvement in the international and domestic economies enables him to write with authority based on his practical experience.